REFRAME 04

NO ART ABOVE POLITICS

TEXTS FOR PHOTOGRAPHERS

RED BOX | 5 x 7 EDITIONS

CONTENTS

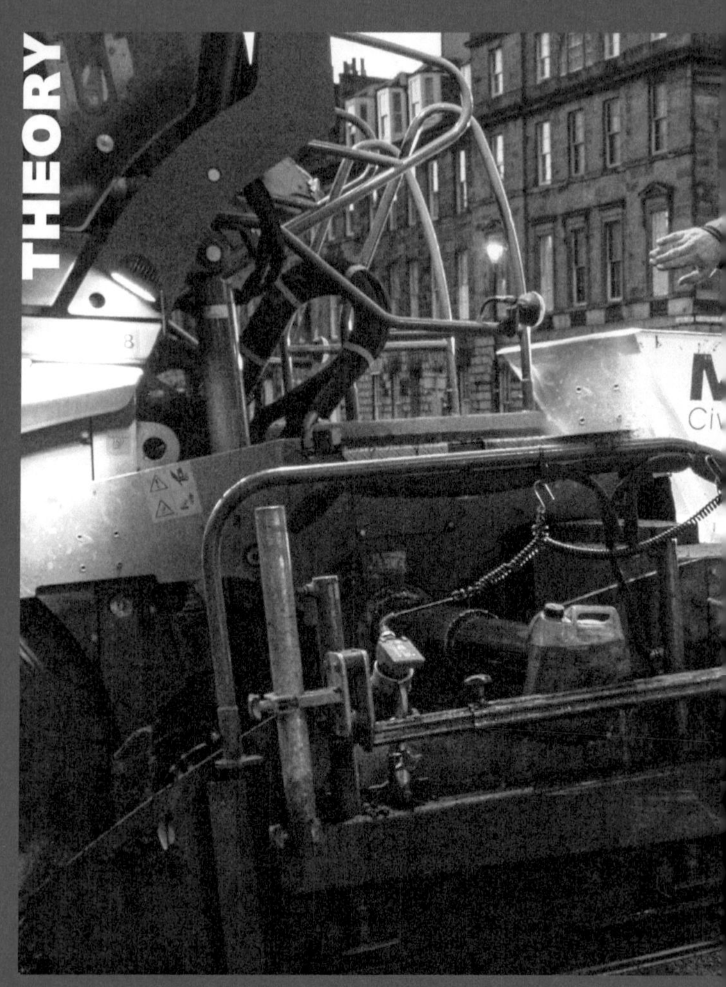

THEORY

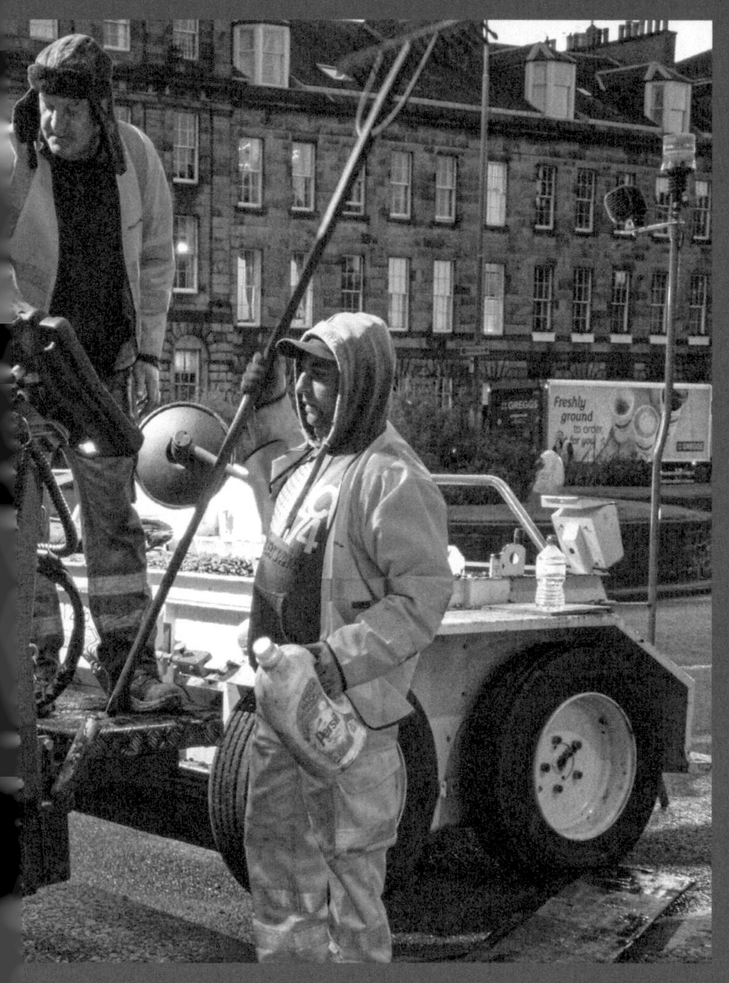
GREGG'S
Freshly
ground
to order
for you
Persil

KARL MARX

THE GERMAN IDEOLOGY

THE IDEAS OF THE RULING CLASS are in every epoch the ruling ideas, i.e. the class which is the ruling material force of society, is at the same time its ruling intellectual force. The class which has the means of material production at its disposal, has control at the same time over the means of mental production, so that thereby, generally speaking, the ideas of those who lack the means of mental production are subject to it. The ruling ideas are nothing more than the ideal expression of the dominant material relationships, the dominant material relationships grasped as ideas.

MAO ZEDONG

TALKS AT THE YENAN FORUM ON LITERATURE AND ART

IN THE WORLD TODAY, all culture, all literature and art belong to definite classes and are geared to definite political lines. There is in fact no such thing as art for art's sake, art that stands above classes, art that is detached from or independent of politics.

WHAT DO WE READ?

How and why do we read?
And how and why does the bourgeoisie read?
The bourgeoisie read for fun, for diversion.
We read to learn, to concentrate.
In their books, the bourgeoisie
seek illusion, escape from reality.
In our books, we seek reality,
so as to change it.
The bourgeoisie want a 'trip', an 'experience'.
We want to stimulate our minds,
broaden our awareness.
For the bourgeoisie, art is for pleasure, for consumption.
For us, art is for thought, for learning, for struggle.

ÁRPÁD SZÉLPÁL

PHOTOGRAPHY AND THE CLASS STRUGGLE

SZOCIALIZMUS, 1931: 5

CAPITALIST SOCIETY converts all elements of its culture, including its fine arts, literature and photography into instruments of class warfare. By misleading and falsifying our vision, either consciously or unconsciously, photographers who do not present the world of phenomena in their true sharpness, harshness and reality but spoil and mislead our vision under the aegis of so-called artistic effects, work to serve this aim.

PARTY ORGANISATION AND PARTY LITERATURE

WE MUST SAY to you bourgeois individualists that your talk about absolute freedom is sheer hypocrisy. There can be no real and effective "freedom" in a society based on the power of money, in a society in which the masses of working people live in poverty and the handful of rich live like parasites. Are you free in relation to your bourgeois publisher, Mr. Writer, in relation to your bourgeois public, which demands that you provide it with pornography in frames and paintings, and prostitution as a "supplement" to "sacred" scenic art? This absolute freedom is a bourgeois phrase. One cannot live in society and be free from society. The freedom of the bourgeois writer, artist or actress is simply masked (or hypocritically masked) dependence on the money-bag, on corruption, on prostitution. And we socialists expose this hypocrisy and rip off the false labels, not in order to arrive at a non-class literature and art, but to contrast this hypocritically free literature, which is in reality linked to the bourgeoisie, with a really free one that will be openly linked to the proletariat. It will be a free literature, because the idea of socialism and sympathy with the working people, and not greed or careerism, will bring ever new forces to its ranks. It will be a free literature, because it will serve, not some satiated heroine, not the bored "upper ten thousand" suffering from fatty degeneration, but the millions and tens of millions of working people.

PRACTICE

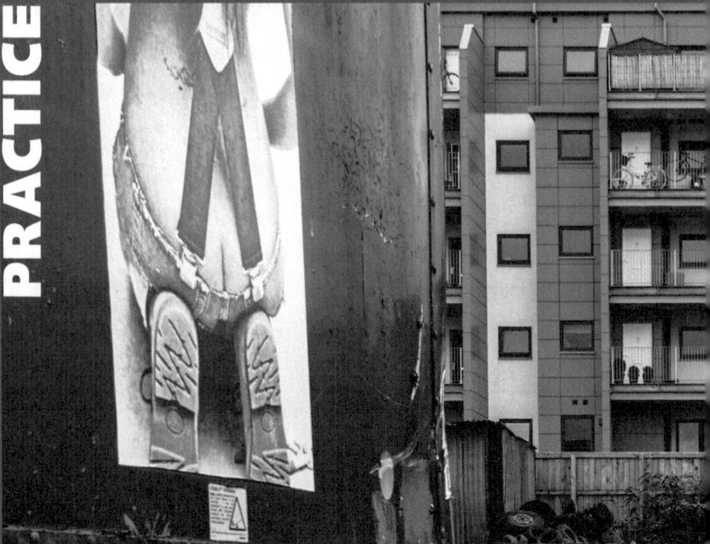

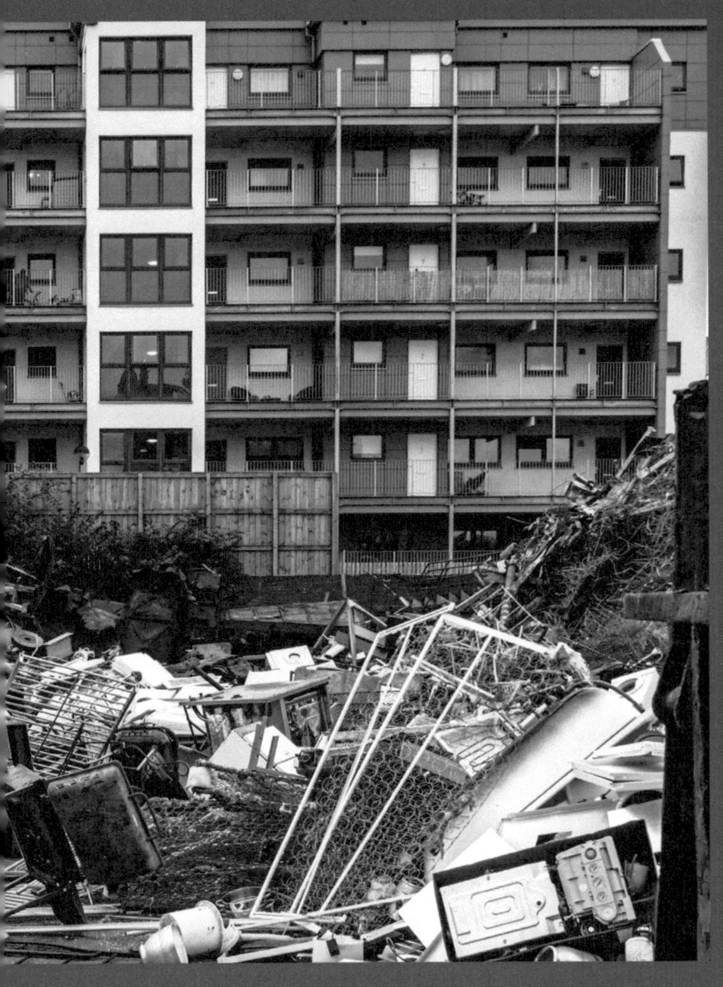

20   NO ART ABOVE POLITICS

CORNELIUS CARDEW

STOCKHAUSEN SERVES IMPERIALISM

LIFE OFFERS many lessons. Mistakes may be turned to advantage. The important thing for us artists and intellectuals is to "move our feet over to the side of the workers". In doing so we may lose that part of our artistry and our intellectuality that is orientated towards bourgeois society and this loss should be celebrated, not bemoaned.

ALLAN SEKULA

DISMANTLING MODERNISM, REINVENTING DOCUMENTARY

PHOTOGRAPHY/POLITICS: ONE

THE ONLY NECESSARY RIGOR in a commodified cultural environment is that of incessant artistic self-promotion. Here elite culture becomes a parasitical "mannerist" representation of mass culture, a private-party sideshow, with its own photojournalism, gossip column reviews, promoters, celebrity pantheon, and narcissistic stellar-bound performers. The charisma of the art star is subject to an overdeveloped bureaucratism. Careers are "managed". Innovation is regularized, adjusted to the demands of the market. Modernism, *per se* (as well as the lingering ghost of bohemianism), is transformed into farce, into a professionalism based on academic appointments, periodic exposure, lofty real estate speculation in the former factory districts of decaying cities, massive state funding, jet travel, and increasingly ostentatious corporate patronage of the arts. This last development represents an attempt by monopoly capital to "humanize" its image for the middle-managerial and professional subclasses (the vicarious consumers of high culture, the museum audience) in the face of an escalating legitimation crisis. High art is rapidly becoming a specialized colony of the monopoly capitalist media.

A small number of contemporary photographers have set out deliberately to work against the strategies that have

ALLAN SEKULA

succeeded in making photography a high art. They insist on treating photographs not as privileged objects but as common cultural artefacts. The solitary, sparely captioned photograph on the gallery wall is a sign, above all, of an aspiration toward the aesthetic and market conditions of modernist painting and sculpture. In this white void, meaning is thought to emerge entirely from within the artwork. The importance of the framing discourse is masked, context is hidden. These artists, on the other hand, openly bracket their photographs with language, using texts to anchor, contradict, reinforce, subvert, complement, particularize, or go beyond the meanings offered by the photographs themselves.

ONE NEEDS the professional eye to pick up at once certain details of landscape or machinery, the clothing or habits of other people; and you need the eye of a certain class in order to perceive the signs of prevailing social conditions in the internal and external life of our fellow human beings, in the structure and appearance of homes and factories, their internal organization and the general picture of life in the streets.

MAO ZEDONG

TALKS AT THE YENAN FORUM ON LITERATURE AND ART

IN LITERARY AND ART CRITICISM there are two criteria, the political and the artistic... There is the political criterion and there is the artistic criterion; what is the relationship between the two? Politics cannot be equated with art, nor can a general world outlook be equated with a method of artistic creation and criticism. We deny not only that there is an abstract and absolutely unchangeable political criterion, but also that there is an abstract and absolutely unchangeable artistic criterion; each class in every class society has its own political and artistic criteria. But all classes in all class societies invariably put the political criterion first and the artistic criterion second... What we demand is the unity of politics and art, the unity of content and form, the unity of revolutionary political content and the highest possible perfection of artistic form. Works of art which lack artistic quality have no force, however progressive they are politically. Therefore, we oppose both works of art with a wrong political viewpoint and the tendency towards the "poster and slogan style" which is correct in political viewpoint but lacking in artistic power. On questions of literature and art we must carry on a struggle on two fronts.

EUGEN HEILIG

MEMORIES OF A WORKER PHOTOGRAPHER

FOTOGRAFIE, 1980:2

FOR US THERE WAS NO ART, technique was a means, not an end. We learned to use the camera as a weapon in the class struggle and quite simply through the most realistic presentation to strive for the highest clarity and expression in photography through simplicity, truthful representation.

POLITICAL PHOTOGRAPHY is hardly being practiced at all. Social photo reportage amounts to little more than pictures of mutilated beggars or figures of misery rummaging through garbage cans. But that is not the issue. The issue is to express a political idea, a social concept in pictorial form. And to accomplish that, one needs both juxtaposition and arresting captions.

WALTER BENJAMIN

THE AUTHOR AS PRODUCER

WHAT WE REQUIRE of the photographer is the ability to give his picture the caption that wrenches it from modish commerce and gives it a revolutionary useful value.

THE WORKERS' WORLD is invisible to the bourgeoisie. If the bourgeoisie depicts proletarians and their world of suffering it is only to provide a contrast, a dark background to set off the glories of bourgeois "culture", "humanity", "arts and sciences" and so forth, so that sensitive folk can enjoy a feeling of sympathy and "compassion" or else take pride in the consciousness of their own superiority. Our photographers must tear down this facade. We must proclaim proletarian reality in all its disgusting ugliness, with its indictment of society and its demand for revenge. We will have no veils, no retouching, no aestheticism; we must present things as they are, in a hard, merciless light. We must take photographs wherever proletarian life is at its hardest and the bourgeoisie at its most corrupt; and we shall increase the fighting power of our class in so far as our pictures show class consciousness, mass consciousness, discipline, solidarity, a spirit of aggression and revenge. Photography is a weapon.

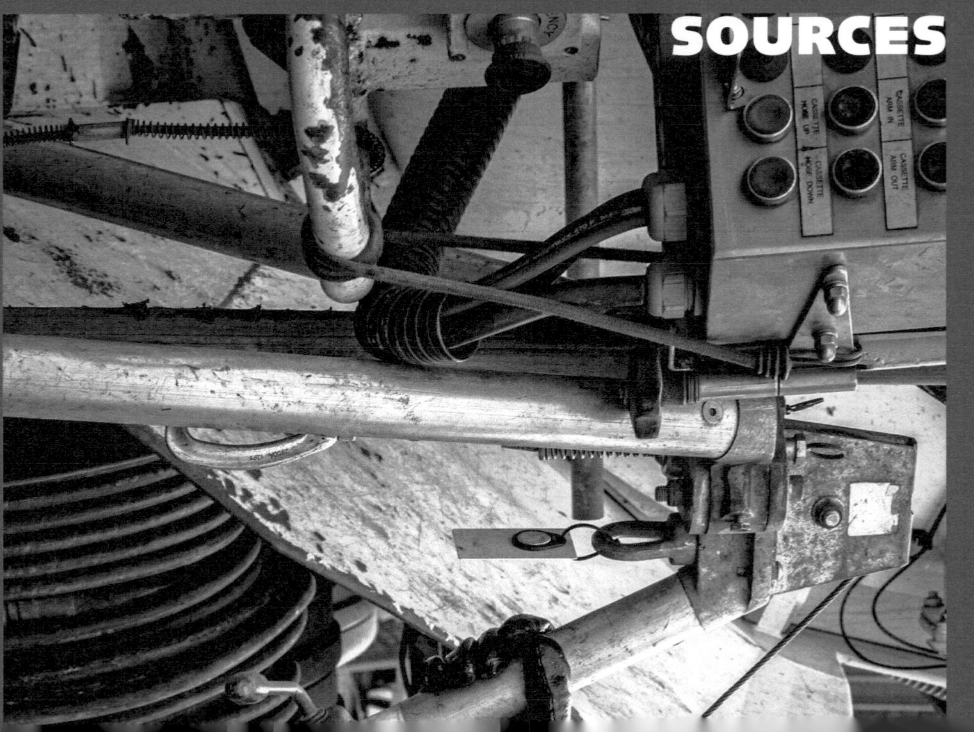
SOURCES
CASSETTE HOSE UP
CASSETTE HOSE DOWN
CASSETTE ARM IN
CASSETTE ARM OUT

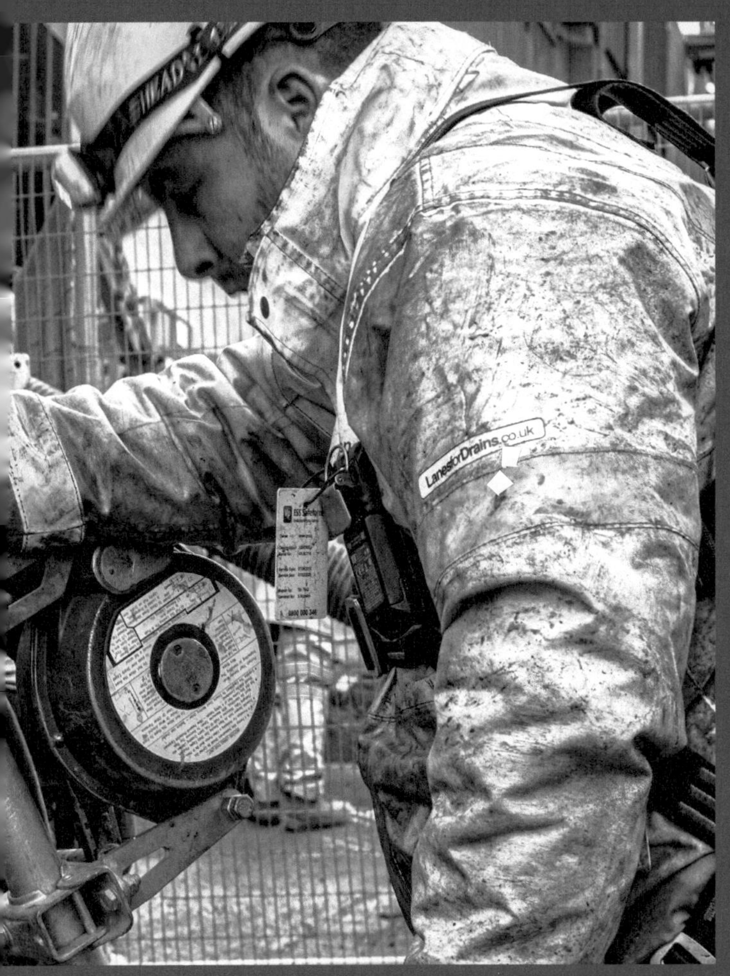

LanesforDrains.co.uk

CAMERA AS WEAPON: WORKER PHOTOGRAPHY BETWEEN THE WARS

  MUSEUM OF PHOTOGRAPHIC ARTS SAN DIEGO, 1991

DAS AUGE DES ARBEITERS SPECTOR BOOKS, 2014

DER ARBEITERFOTOGRAF ARBEITERFOTOGRAFIE.COM

EDITH TUDOR-HART: IN THE SHADOW OF TYRANNY HATJE CANTZ, 2013

EDITH TUDOR-HART: THE EYE OF CONSCIENCE DIRK NISHEN PUBLISHING, 1987

FOTOGRAFIE IM KLASSENKAMPF VEB FOTOKINOVERLAG, 1981

MAO TSE-TUNG ON LITERATURE AND ART FOREIGN LANGUAGES PRESS, 1967

NOT YET: ON THE REINVENTION OF DOCUMENTARY AND THE CRITIQUE

  OF MODERNISM: ESSAYS AND DOCUMENTS (1972-1991)

  MUSEO NACIONAL CENTRO DE ARTE REINA SOFÍA, 2015

PHOTOGRAPHIE: ARME DE CLASSE TEXTUEL, 2018

PHOTOGRAPHY AGAINST THE GRAIN MACK, 2016

PHOTOGRAPHY/POLITICS: ONE PHOTOGRAPHY WORKSHOP, 1979

STOCKHAUSEN SERVES IMPERIALISM PRIMARY INFORMATION, 2020

THE POWER OF PICTURES: EARLY SOVIET PHOTOGRAPHY, EARLY SOVIET FILM

  THE JEWISH MUSEUM NEW YORK, 2015

THE RADICAL CAMERA: NEW YORK'S PHOTO LEAGUE 1936-1951

  YALE UNIVERSITY PRESS, 2012

THE WORKER-PHOTOGRAPHY MOVEMENT 1926-1939 T F EDITORES, 2011

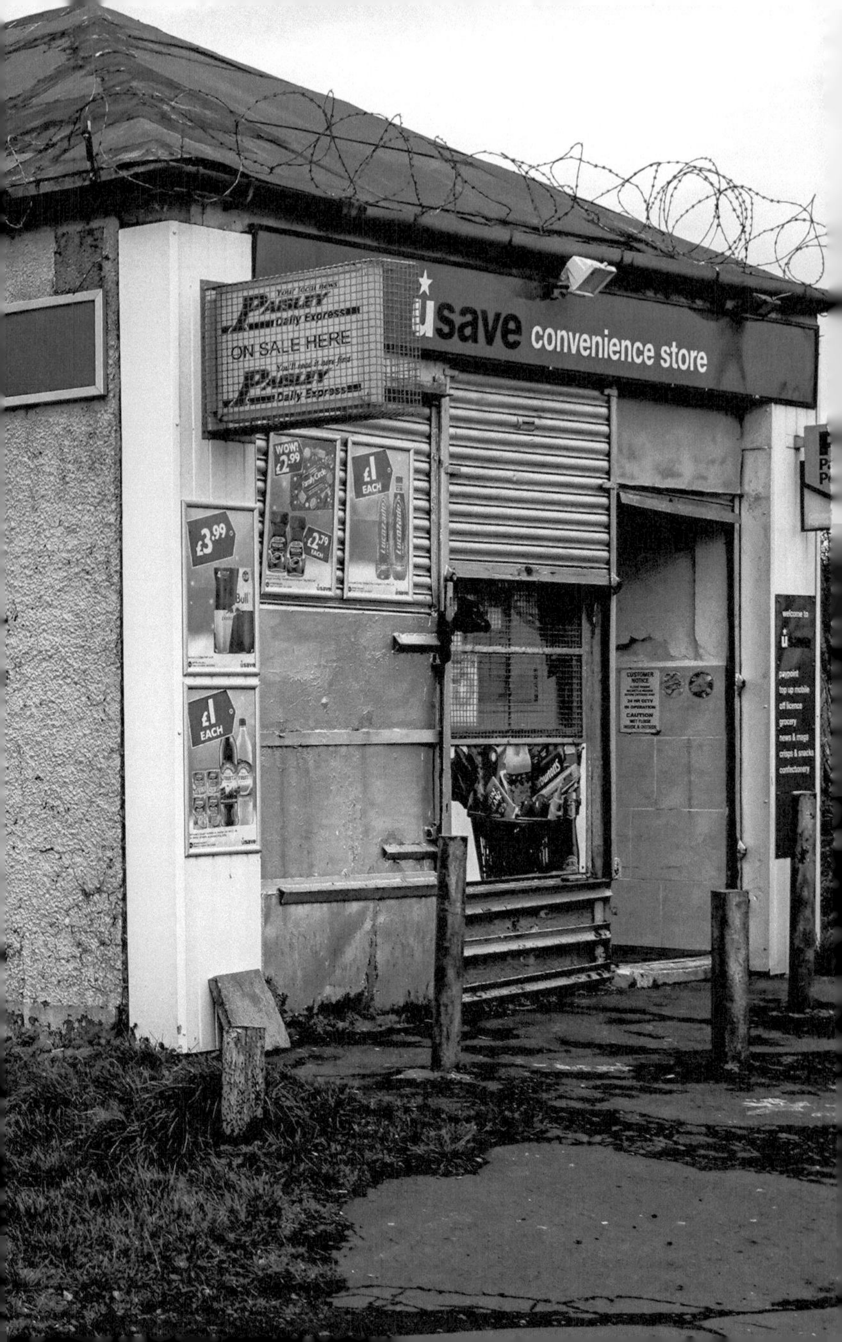

Your local news
PAISLEY Daily Express
ON SALE HERE
You'll read it here first
PAISLEY Daily Express
usave convenience store
WOW! £2.99
Family Circle
£1 EACH
£3.99
Bull
£2.79 EACH
£1 EACH
welcome to
u
paypoint
top up mobile
off licence
grocery
news & mags
crisps & snacks
confectionery
CUSTOMER NOTICE
24 HR CCTV
IN OPERATION
CAUTION
WET FLOOR
INSIDE & OUTSIDE

THE REFRAME COLLECTION

isbn 978-1-912528-36-3
edition ©2023 5 × 7 editions
images ©red box
www.5x7editions.com

the paper used in printing this book comes from responsibly managed
forests and meets the requirements of the forest stewardship council™